COLLAGE OF SEOUL

The Poiema Poetry Series

Poems are windows into worlds; windows into beauty, goodness, and truth; windows into understandings that won't twist themselves into tidy dogmatic statements; windows into experiences. We can do more than merely peer into such windows; with a little effort we can fling open the casements, and leap over the sills into the heart of these worlds. We are also led into familiar places of hurt, confusion, and disappointment, but we arrive in the poet's company. Poetry is a partnership between poet and reader, seeking together to gain something of value—to get at something important.

Ephesians 2:10 says, "We are God's workmanship . . ." *poiema* in Greek— the thing that has been made, the masterpiece, the poem. The Poiema Poetry Series presents the work of gifted poets who take Christian faith seriously, and demonstrate in whose image we have been made through their creativity and craftsmanship.

These poets are recent participants in the ancient tradition of David, Asaph, Isaiah, and John the Revelator. The thread can be followed through the centuries—through the diverse poetic visions of Dante, Bernard of Clairvaux, Donne, Herbert, Milton, Hopkins, Eliot, R. S. Thomas, and Denise Levertov—down to the poet whose work is in your hand. With the selection of this volume you are entering this enduring tradition, and as a reader contributing to it.

—D.S. Martin
Series Editor

Collage of Seoul

Poems by

JAE NEWMAN

CASCADE *Books* · Eugene, Oregon

COLLAGE OF SEOUL

The Poiema Poetry Series

Cascade
An Imprint of Wipf and Stock Publishers
199 W. 8th Ave., Suite 3
Eugene, OR 97401

www.wipfandstock.com

ISBN 13: 978-1-4982-0724-9

Cataloging-in-Publication data:

Jae Newman.

    Collage of Seoul / Jae Newman.

    88 p.; 23 cm—Includes bibliographical references and index.

    The Poiema Poetry Series

    ISBN 13: 978-1-4982-0724-9

    1. American Poetry—21st Century I. Title II. Series

PS3725.A237 2015

Manufactured in the USA.

For Natasha

Contents

Contents

Loran

I never needed to find myself.
They did a good job at the orphanage.

Scooped up all my pieces, tied them
tightly with a cub scout knot.

It came as a surprise, one night,
to hear my heart create a second beat.

Listening on a stethoscope, I heard
its space: a limpid muscle, likely dead.

Even so, the loran, it ached. Like any explorer,
I know naming is part of the job.

Charting without genes, without you,
I find it hard to trust the maps and stars

of other men. If I follow anything,
may it be the sound I cannot hear,

the feeling causing me to stand, the needle
blistering back and forth

as we meet behind my river nerve:
a thousand candles floating in paper boats.

I.

Apartment Near Airport

Soft words folded into envelopes of prayer.
The dogs hear it first.

Not my prayer, but the sound
of shadows in the neighboring trees.

I can feel the shadow of the engine
before I hear it.

Body at rest, I wrestle with God,
nurse wounds in the dark.

Bracing for the heavy presence of the plane,
I cringe in its sound, crawl out

holding wings while steel hips rust
to reveal a man who was never a child,

a man who wanders airports alone at night
attracted to the ebb and flow of runways,

where beneath the grindings of identity,
there's comfort in the fading echo,

the tail of the plane vanishing
into layers of mysterious clouds.

Unnamed

To know you never named me is to know
why I must name my life away in words, in waiting.

I went to the library, one day, and traced a peninsula,
Korea, into my sketch book.

I wonder if, later, you ever picked a name for me
while doing household chores,

hanging clothes along the Han River shore, or maybe
walking home from the port

with a bag full of fish, and soap
to wash your hands of burying my name in dirt.

Mother Tree

I am free
       cut loose from
the branches of the Mother Tree,
surrendered
to the fostered fingers of a silver bird.

I was nine
       when I found you, planted,
arms part of an unreachable sky.

Running alone at dusk,
I cried for your attention

       the single time in my life

pointing at a bloody shin.
I wanted you to see

what a snapped-back branch had done to me.

On a hill in the woods, I wiped blood away
until all the leaves were red, then

stood up, your roots quivering
as I kissed the bark, gripped an ax.

Pushing Chi

If these hands cannot conceive
what I see,

cannot understand his left
from mine, then

I exist in compromise
alone.

I have not come this far
in self-definition

to risk it all on one move,
but my spirit

knows why I must try.
Here I am, directing

two forces in opposition:
push and pull.

I know this. I am this
and yet,

I struggle to keep pace,
a move behind

the man on a video,
a master

whose breath is invisible,
if taken at all.

Aureole

This same poem, unsaid,
in a thousand lonely mouths,
each holding a pencil
torching lead love letters

in long, arching graphite rainbows.
Jasmine leaves shade the light
but when the sun sets,
when everything is dark,

when my eyes are worthless,
my heaven is always only
an inch away from the world.
It is the distance my fingers travel

when I touch your spine,
the center of the universe,
reciting those archaic words, *I love you*.
Adrenal ash spread over the lip

of a blue flame; love; water
on the orchid of wanting
to be found and clipped by you.
This vase, Pyrex, is a bed, of course,

as my hand, lost in the tectonics of your back,
removes the cosmos with my daily trespass,
as fingers climb that little mountain
where enlightenment is held in an open box

by Aurora, who greets me coldly,
in white gloves. Even a goddess knows
that her hands are not fit to hold my love of you,
the words of a love child

closing the distance of a god
down to the length of a ring finger.

Postage

Leafing through pages
    of a phone book in dream,

I cut my tongue on a Korean War stamp
before noticing

    a million of them,

spilling from the blackness of a woman's purse.

Collage of Seoul

Taped over the headboard, eleven photos
of her neckline
                    a river splashing through
the wound.

Framed in a golden tomb, the cries of my mother
freeze most specks of traffic.
                              Tiny cars

pass over bridges, some
never return.

Adrift

Cottonwood in static suspension—
it covers the neighbor's lawn.

Mid-May, we talk of moving
again. She says we should stay
and I always want to go
somewhere new
and redefine ourselves perpetually
as newlyweds, as
the couple who can not
see its shadow.

Outside the window, floating in the air
the whispers of dead dandelions
mowed down
reminds me of another time,
another spring
before I had allergies
when staring at strange snow falling up
might have touched the chord,
an echo on my spine.

Hikikomori

If a plant cannot live according to its nature, it dies; and so a man.
–Thoreau

Following blue footprints
painted on cold sidewalks,

I disappeared behind an old hospital.
Laying on a white H,

I searched the sky
for helicopters or falling stars.

Removing shards of parental debris,
I covered my torso in snow,

buried what sought translation, escaped
a body I never wanted

or felt was mine. It's easy to mistake
electricity as light. Harder

to convince a flower it's fine,
a lamp is the sun.

There are one hundred twelve varieties of the lie
and I am not above a few.

How many clung to me as I stood?
Drawn toward a playground,

I touched chains upholding swings,
set metal in motion.

I have no business being here.

Land of the Morning Calm

There is no want in me but for you:
drag a honeycomb through my hair,
deaden all thoughts of dismantling
this stinger in my spine. Mother,

they bleached you into obscurity. Infants
don't fly, and so, you painted stripes on me,
made me a Korean bee with a quiet stinger
to help me collide with the Yellow Sea.

When I am torn up about who I am,
I take comfort where comfort stings,
sit alone at sunset watching a black sky
swallow tiny silver planes, but nothing

can keep me from swarming the aviary,
a Buddhist bumblebee in the dead of February.

One Hundred Words for Snow

I whisper *Yhwh* against a rage
that has cost me more than fingers and toes.
I could not hold, bury, or escape
the shape of your grief. It moved
along glaciers snapping the ends
of islands into the sea.

Lips pressed to sleeve, I carried
mouthfuls of your dust mumbling dead prayer,
prayers made and lost within the solitude
of imagined Alaskan parks where
I chased your sorrow only to discover
the land where mine is local legend.

Vanishing woman, the way to the Bering Strait
is lined with lessons of your winter.
I travel by foot against evidence
of sinking islands, of shadowy disappearances.
I travel alone because the land of
one hundred words for snow is not your hell:
it's mine.

Permission

It is one of those times when I understand
I must become my own church, or

feel my mother's estrogen move through
sunlight into the density of bones.

I follow a solitary flame toward love.

This candle, on the floor,
the less it dances, the more I want you.

You say that artists must be mad
to be real artists. If I am a fraud, only

a man who writes love poems, then
you're only an ordinary woman.

Sitting here in our kitchen, it is darkness
but for this vulnerable candle.

Of God songs, of praising in this Pollock pattern
of wordless sense,

I find a crumpled petal among crumbs.

I have buried my eyelids, stalked shores for your body,
shattered walls with concentration. I have

been mad once, and would prefer not to be again.

Straddling this line, I want you to have everything of me,
and this includes my mind.

My voice has never been enough light to help you, but
its sound is a candle and candles exist only for light.

II.

Negative

Tell me again—
your shadow
is really just
my absence in light.
In the shower,
lost between
woman and water,
I wait to rinse
my hair. Turning
with closed eyes,
all I can sense
is what's
immeasurable:

—beautiful darkness,
contained void,
its slender shape
floating across
a curtain of light,
erasing her absence
with a towel
before mine
can be missed.

Doors Among Trees

Lost on your childhood trail

      we came upon hundreds of doors leaning against trees

scattered in an Alleghany abstract of strange colors

with wood chipped into splintered echoes

      the windows missing as the thought of being lost
was lost

      and replaced with the childish awe of a fantasia world

as if our bodies weren't just pushing through brush
                           looking for the road

but in search of something holy
                  something hidden
in the foothills.

Reincarnation

Hovering in dangerous friction,

the dry skin of my fingers
is kindling again

in the static fire of your hair.

I don't believe in reincarnation, but
I'm almost there.

Perhaps, there was a second garden
in Eden

where intervals of stony darkness
have always been disrupted

by an unutterable light, a prism

I planted once
in the darkest roots of your hair.

Two Thousand Lilacs

1.

Spiraling toward the sound of water, I could not lead,
confused by the park map. Climbing the gentle slopes,
among budding lilacs, I found myself
                                        trying to understand
what is common to us, what brought thousands
to walk these paved paths immersed in lilac. Moving
                                        in rhythm,
with your hand enclosed in mine, you told me
there was a top to this hill, a place to look and see the city
                                        in which we live.
I could not lead, and direction confused you
at least once or twice that afternoon. Lost
among pine trees, you unbuttoned your denim shirt
then removed it
                        revealing your shoulders
against the sun for the first time all summer. Later that evening
I collected the lilac salts that clung
to your collarbone,
as thirst idles, as we whispered old songs,
shadows taut in aching prayer.

2.

Kissing in the shadow of your spine, I trailed a few steps behind,
admiring you,
        a flower, the only one I touched.
Kissing in the shadow of your spine, I was conscious
of my mind absorbed in scenery—

                        heaven, anonymity,
a comfort for lovers like us. I don't know how this happened, or

why I envisioned entering heaven as something like spiraling that hill,
but I found myself memorizing everything—
                                   a bird's song, tiny birthmarks,
constellations on your shoulders,
                                   the sound of water.
Later, as my lips traveled up vertebrae,
I pictured you walking ahead
reaching your hand back to me as we ascended the final set of stairs.
Later, my lips worked up your back,
                         beneath your clothes, beneath your name.

   3.

Holding you as we descend into sleep, the scent of purple petals
                              remain in my nose and mind. It is dark
and I can't see anything but the shadow

of your body. I inch there, pinching petals with open palms,
                                   refusing to end the day.
Drifting back a week, I think of your mother's mother
                                   walking
the paths we did, her steps recorded on eight mm film. Silent, black
and white,
the images unfold: her smile breaking through bushes and trees, the way
your grandfather loved
                    to be in the way of the camera.
Wandering back to Highland Park, my mind
                    thinks it's found a way to preserve this day:
delay night.

   4.
How many times did we see that little barefoot boy? His dark skin, a
fire,
        a voice, an angel? Running through the paths,
he was an orphan
                    without knowledge of his mother. We know
each other, we who were never breastfed.

5.

Returning to the darkness of our bedroom, I turn from you
so I can sleep. I can't face you and forgive myself for ending
such a sweet day. Not touching you, I wander past a pantheon of faces
only to break their
hearts.
I break their hearts
only to show you
that you're my country, my Seoul,
my wreckage.
I remember the way I felt when your shoulders crushed the sun—
how your lemonade was sour for lacking water,
how that little barefoot boy looked at us,
how wonderful it felt to be lost
in this city, its tiny buildings rumbling in the distance.

6.

In this darkroom, I hang pictures for you.
I am sorry
that I cannot lead us to heaven—you will have to do that, but
I will remember
napping under trees,
walking through a park holding hands,
holding centuries of pain
between palms
as we kissed on bridges whose structures could
never hold
the wildness of our love.
I don't know why
this lifetime
is made of molecules of suffering.
I don't know why I handed you the lyre, and
can't say why I ask you to put bandages over all my cuts, those healed
scars.
I carried you, a snake-bitten bride,
and your song

over the gaze of disbelievers
who could not understand how we were tapped by clouds,
draped with affections we
neither knew of
nor could do without.
With affections so deep
I am sure enough I am a man alive
two thousand years after The Way was made,
two thousand lilacs
enough
to need nothing
but your body over mine.

Passports

We had them expedited to be sure.
We were going.

When I am alone

sometimes I open our fire-proof box

and look at our passports, set them
on the sofa,

and think about living in Korea. The week

we had our photos
taken, we went to Wal-Mart

to find the Photo Department under
construction.

I carried the envelope with my identity:
the orphan photo, the legalese,

the Naturalization papers

that gave me my name. Photocopied ghost,

who are you? Boy who hated wool sweaters,

I saw my passport photo
and let go. Late spring,

I made small chat with the photographer, a man
whose eyes no longer flinched

at the sound of a drill blaming concrete.

Word

Already, before you are born,
your mother asleep, I work
on your vocabulary. Child,
you are the word, the mutable truth
I have always sought to know,
the whisper that makes men blush,
the reason why women
endure sea sick months to hold
the diamond that turns a womb
into an orchard in heavenly bloom.

*

This is your father. You are developing lungs
this week, but for now
just listen.

As I hold your mother's belly beneath the waist
of dark jeans
she's putting some mascara on.

Sensing you, child, my brokenness knows
it no longer matters.

Healing, it is a song vibrating silently
as I kiss your mother's neck.

River

Here, in this bed, I am the eastern bank
and my wife is the west. Here,
my daughter is the river who flows backwards
against time, who undoes knots she never knew of,
and unsays what I denied, deny, or will.
Here, twisting,
just beyond the moment where my back goes numb,
where the new parent prays
for one hour of uninterrupted sleep,
I wade into dream alone.

                *

There are rivers where we're meant to fish alone,
places where no one can distract a bent ear
that hears nothing but a thread of water. Waist-deep
in what I believe—what I don't believe
wants to rise up, break free into scatterings
of limitless flight. In case I forget,
the river knows my name. I am a man with no lure
and a whispery line that never catches
what it seeks. O heart, O empty drum
whose skin's pulled taut, you have never asked
the right questions. You have always spoken
when reflection was enough, suffocated love
you neither could live with nor without.
Rising in the water, glistening,
a giant fish flies up piercing a blue sky
before crashing into the waking world
as my daughter's hand taps my forehead,
the fish still flopping as her eyes find mine.

First Slow Dance with My Daughter

After nine months in her mother's womb
she can't quite fathom

where her body begins or where
mine ends. Arms flail in need

of speech, her head
rotating, restless, in search of wordless

answers. Moving between rooms
in the dark, we sway

to the sound of a single flute,
soothing music meant to relax

her. Or maybe it's for me,
this one-winged melody

spinning us further and further apart
as she drifts back to sleep.

She does not need me. What
can I give? A father

I dance in the shadows, up
now for a third time. Humming

along, I'm afraid
that if I pull her closer,

cheek to cheek,
she will startle and remember

she has a body.

Artifacts

Before you officially become you, before
you begin the long road north
to be nothing
like your mother or father, let me
leave this map,
a stained glass song
lit up across the longest night
of your life.

*

The truth is
there is no truth but for the Lord. Everything
is fantasy, a maze
where what you want
is veiled in the hard rain of painted borders
you cannot cross.

*

Let me do a simple thing for you.
This string from my heart, it sings
to your mother and now to you. Hold
its song in a jar, for what is lost
is lost forever, and what disappears
between us will be ransomed
in the place where you will be royalty,
where garlands of memory
are hung in your honor.

*

Before you dismiss me, before I embarrass you,
as all fathers do, mind this:

from my father, the man who shot himself out of a cannon
and never returned,

I would listen to a thousand jokes I never liked;
I would wear his clothes and watch as others wondered
why our suit pants were rolled at the knee.

Marriage

This is not the first
or last time
I submit to the force that draws me
closer to her, the cost
be damned. Driving
before sunrise
on the way to work,
we're the only two cars
on 394 heading west. I know
there's no way
I could stop, and
the fog advisory should
mean something to me,
my car inching closer
to her car, needing
to be closer, to say
something unspoken,
in love, unafraid
of collision.

Our spines, quivering,
we do not control
the magnetic song
we recognize anywhere,
the one that brings me
close to tears, the one
where the sound of danger
makes us smile,
the one where risk
is implied in the vow.

City of Light

1.

When you are still,
adrift in that deepest flora
of sleep, I find it harder
now not to wake you,
to deny you extra minutes
of rest because
those minutes are
hours and hours
are days we won't
get back. We are not teenagers,
my love, and you know that.
It's why I'm desperate
to make something up to you
I never will.

2.

Awake, a husband dreams
of a new theology
where your hair is the Word
and his hand is the mouth
to set the world
ablaze. If our bodies
aren't sacred, only
wine skins for a spirit,
why is each hair
counted in heaven's cartel?
And why am I quivering?
My hand
almost touching you,
nervous of your beauty
ten years later.

3.

Laying in your shadow,
if only this was all
the world expected of me. If
only being here,
loyal, yours, was enough
to extinguish the flames
rising around us.

4.

Play your fingers down
the center of my spine. For you
I will do the same. Such notes
engrain the song we'll one day play,
our memories blasted forth.
Cross the spectrum of my being
to where I am not,
to the small series of pews
in the forest I return to
within sleep's song,
only to seek your perfume,
the scent of vanilla,
a lucid flare from your collarbone
at eighteen when
you tutored me in kissing.

5.

Whispers are gunfire here
in the land where words are outlawed,
in the land where I am wanted
for counts of blasphemy,
where I have wrestled God
to ensure we are together.
Where I've been
I would not call sleep, but

something close. If heaven is mute,
a place where pronouns,
stories and answers are obsolete,
then let me etch what's known
below. Wholeness
is a damned thing. So break me, my love,
break me into pieces
because they all belong to you.

6.

If we find ourselves apart one day
as glimmers of the same light,
bodiless and still pulled toward
each other, turn your glow
down, off, so that we will
find each other, lonely,
two nebulae stumbling about
a city of light.

III.

Canticle

If I handed you everything, my life
in colorless newspaper font,

and asked you to dip it in papier-mâché
made of paint, mercury, saliva, and glue,

would you, a stranger, be my Samaritan
and layer thin dripping strips

upon this miraculous breath of mine?
Guarding a balloon with closed lips, if

I am called to speak now, friend,
can I trust you? O Lord

I have asked and received so many times,
I forget he cannot turn to you who cannot hear

the dark song that needs no introduction.
Perhaps, only the quiet one among friends,

the one who stays in at night,
can watch the glow of heavenly optics moving

through space, lucid music colliding now
with the echo of a single word you know

but won't say.

Hives

               Be-
cause sometime in April,
you reached for a phone. Be-

cause I spent six weeks in your shadow.
          Because you sang to me,
but made no promises. Because
          you carried me, one morning,
on an empty bus. Because
          you wouldn't look at me. Because
when the doors opened
          you burst into tears. Because
I was an infant and you
          were my mother. Because
you told everyone to go
          to hell. Because you already knew
hell was a kingdom too,
          hidden within. Because my name
was nothing: baby. Because
          I continue to daydream and can't
be trusted on the road. Because
          you said things I never understood.
Because my dependence on English
          is as good as I can do. Because
I expect that much of you. Because
          I am a father now. Because
you are a grandmother. Because
          time zones, words, and doors,
couldn't contain me. Because
          this is fiction. Because I am non-fiction,
a black blanket stretched overhead,
          a set of twenty questions,
stars I whittled down to one.

Sea Woman

When I learned you lived in Jeju Island,

    the honeymooner's paradise,

I knew it all. Your hands as dry irons,

    you worked each day tending

simple tasks: wash, rinse. Weeks before we met,

    I prayed I was wrong. Prayed

you were a Haenyo, a woman who dove

    into frigid waters without scuba gear

to pull forth a living. I pictured you alone

    all these years diving through shades of purple

and blue, my birth a heavy stone

    unearthed while raking through seaweed glass.

Jagged mosaic, here I am

    lifted against mussel and clam into a mesh bag

before rising from time to time,

    a memory of that year, a bubble

no hypothermic shock could kill.

Album

Sunday, up early, I'm missing church
alone in a pharmacy. Only the clerk is here
to help me scan photos.

Sliding each photo upon its aged face,
it's my life in twenty pictures.

Thinking of meeting my birth mother,
I can't decide if I belong. Deleting photos,
I add them again

unsure how much is needed,
how much is necessary to share.

Breaking News

November 23, 2010

Walking trails at night around an ancient garden,

    it's cold. Korea in November,

I did not bring a coat or hat. Up ahead

    the group has stopped to take pictures.

Steam rises over water lit by lanterns

    as teal beams blaze above us

in these refurbished gazebos, in this illusory garden

    where birds and flowers

once flourished. Heading back to the warmth of the bus,

    the news is gunfire, everyone afraid to ask

what no one wants to know.

Windsock

It starts inside the chest. Hiss
zipping from deep in one's lungs
in search of a way out. Lost

for years in a nylon shell,
mine is the heart that believed
love must be both particle and wave,

that, upon seeing a woman of
a certain age always stood still,
sure she was my mother.

A silent witness, *want* never
denies darkness. And when
the soul constricts on what it targets,

you have to break its spine.
Slap its coil against a tree
until fermented prayers release

snarling in the cool of the grass,
orange shed thrashing
until all ribs are broken.

Jade Pin

Seoul, 2010

We walk from shop to shop, nodding
      as the translator picks up another silk purse.
We walk from shop to shop, nodding
      because my mother wants to buy presents.
When I find a jade pin, its foreign price
      is revealed in my mother's face: *too much.*
As the translator picks up another silk purse,
      we walk from shop to shop, nodding.

Story Told Over Plum Tea

She met him on the street years later.
They stood frozen,

the man and my mother,
before turning away

as though they did not know each other,
as though nothing had happened,

as though the love of her life
meant nothing except

I was gone.

Reflex

As a man on a motor bike brushes by
I reach for her,
unsure if she sees
him. We've met one hour before
and now stroll through Insadong,
a market in Seoul,
to find a gift for my daughter.
I watch my mother's eyes dart
back and forth. Hanboks
and paper fans. There it goes

a moment where touching her shoulder
may have made sense, may have
wakened a reflex she neither could protest
nor retract: a slow-motion clasp
of her hand reaching for mine.

*

Moments later,
there she goes down the platform of a subway,
my hand reaching
for yours.

Visions

Lend me what a father owes his son.

It's easier if I picture you in America, in some dirty city
wearing a brown suit, shouting to an invisible tech crew to hurry.

I have gone into hotels looking for you.

Tried to see your face but it's always blurred, always just
another variation of cinematic suspense where something is broken.

When I realized you weren't that man in that certain suit,

the one I made up in dreams with long hair touching his collar,
that these fabled films were my California sets, I ignored what I knew.

I told myself *this father feels real* when the film is rolling. The film is rolling.

I have imagined what your wedding would have been like,
pretended it was your hand feeding me yellow cake with waxed icing.

Voiceless bravado, I know it's you calling me into dreams with cakes on fire.

Like any unknown son, I formed the bond for us. You and I
sitting in a park was always a durable lie. When I was ready

I had visions of eating all your wedding cake, sitting alone

in an empty hotel ballroom, stuffing my mouth full of grace
then leaving, closing the door.

Heading Westward at 495 MPH

Heading home over the Pacific, our legs
bound by right angles, we did not speak.
Tilted seats folded knees back,
I could not sleep or recline: red eye.

No watch could compass muted time.

On the monitor a small plane icon
floats along its dotted line. Flying
in a gradual arc, its speed in flux,
the Captain says we've got a tail wind,
whipping us back into the past.

Here, on a Saturday we split into two,

I mark time for you. Watching you within
the womb, I just have peanuts. This theater
is crowded, but with your mother asleep,
we listen to the slap of wind and cabin

as movie after movie plays in loop,

borrowed headphones feeding
sound through skin, blood, and water
until we realize we're the only ones awake,
our flight's drifting toward order, on time,
neither wanting to be late.

IV.

Wired Jaw

Honey-laced flytrap,
it isn't your fault you are broken
or that words started coming here

to die. At rest in my mouth,
old grievances bumble through
final testimonies, fully aware

this is it, this is where what was urgent
or deliberate will sound
the same as what is already forgotten.

Here, in the garden of memory,
we can bury what we'd not say
beneath what we said

and wish we had not. Flash a light
inside past these bleeding gums.
Look hard past the rot.

Is there a holy word gaining shape,
an inaudible reply? I heard
my name before the vow,

heard it said one last time
by the voice I loved most
then hurt slightly, as its erasure

confirmed my namelessness. Wired jaw,
shatter! Let everyone hear
this voice now for the first time,

let them ask, *Isn't he the man*
whose lips blurred
like blades of swaying grass?

Isn't he the man whose mumbling
causes waitresses to lean in?
My broken stereophonics restored

these words—hallelujah!—
still vibrate, still glow.

Thy Kingdom Come

Burning for half-an-hour in dry heat,
the grill is ready. Just outside the back door

it's summer. Questions cease,

retire into billows of white smoke.
A new hobby, I burn everything.

Spraying oil over blackened bars, I coax

orange manes bursting in crescendo.
Against the flint of an old prayer

words leap up towards the yellow can.

Flowing towards the source,
fire climbing the ladder to the point

where my finger should let go
but won't.

Under a Hat at the Beach

The red brim of my visor—
set against a clear blue day.

I lay on a towel;
my lover's hand sweats

in mine. Adjusting shoulders
in deep sand

I am alive. Beneath a cloudless sky,

I count blessings.
As blood tumbles free

two girls sing to me.

Blue Periods

1.

There was a time when everything Pablo painted
was in blues.

Poor, desolate, warring with father,

his bearded self-portrait said something.
He was cold.

Out of exile, I heard my name. Not

the one the world knows, but a hushed whisper
traveling across

a no man's land of self-indulgence. Indulging
in women, Pablo

painted them, his lovers, as monsters,

ghostly souls incarcerated in skin and
dark hair.

I call on the Lord, ask

to be hidden in the shadows of trees. Digging
my way through the earth, I find

my fingers are blunt, metal objects

that move through rock, through clay,
through lie and Juche. Slight of build,

I don't care. I've got your divine mandate

right here.

2.

How shall I spread the Word

when the Word is *love* and needs translation?
How does one break a cycle?

Slash and burn?

Elijah called upon the Lord, said,
"Let this boy's life return"

and of course it did. Of course

I could say
I've felt like a puppet, a boy bound by string,

arms, legs, and mouth moving

almost like a real boy.
A real boy is something I can't quite fathom,

can't quite reach.

It is how a man feels when he thinks of Eden,
thinks of the Tree,

thinks of the Lord's breath

hovering the darkened seas. *Let there be light*,
a whisper said.

Can I do that?

Can I learn to whisper?
Learn to be present in the absence of action?

3.

If Adam and Eve had the will to forsake Eden,
to open a box,

then why can't someone return to close it?
For me, all blackness is the same.

If I come from a man, as biology says,
then prove it.

If I come from sperm and egg, prove it.

Show me the hand that charmed a cheek.
Show me that love exists and that sex

isn't just another way unity won't work.
Angel, I am waiting.

Histories conceal our perfect lies.
How can I attack a hermetic pride?

Slash and burn?

Mighty is the Lord whose hands
hold an infinite number of bombs,

little sneezes bursting in palms. He,
who holds my sorrow in the wind. He,

who loves the hungry, the farmer,
the fisherman eating his ration of rice.

4.

There was a time when everything Pablo painted
was in blues. Fishermen standing,

marveling at the blue shore.

I cannot say that this blue is the same.
Sadness is personal, a fleeting stone whose ripples

do not flow evenly.

To change the face of his art, Pablo removed
his heart,

wrapped it in newspaper,
tucked his shame in the shallowness of ego.

How could one man love himself so?

Who can accept the joylessness of children?
Brilliant or not,

art is not enough. It never has been.
Creation bored the lovers

who walked with God through morning

into this dawn where we exist, we think,
in a sort of litmus test.

I don't care what the poem wants.

I want to take the children of North Korea
food shopping.

Let them each have a cart,

open boxes of chocolates,
eat grapes right out of the bags,

let them try every kind of cookie.

Grace unites me to you and him to us.
It isn't my law: forgiveness.

It is not my way.

My father says I hold on to grudges.
That is true.

But what's a grudge but love denied?

And what's love denied but love saved
for eternity,

for one woman, for all time?

Song: Decade

Just a stone's throw from Buffalo
        it's snowing. Out the window
it's nearly nine

and the landlord isn't coming. Under
        my breath, a plastic shovel cracks
in half. Gazing

down the driveway,
        I see the small slivered path my mother
spilled aside. And though my fingers

can't tell what's flesh, what's handle,
        I stop, consider our measures of love
and how work done just hours before

is so often undone in memory: how
        snow sifts across in weightless animation:
how what was radioactive in me defined me

for a decade: how shoveling my driveway
        she'd awaken her fractured hand
because this is love as I understand.

Paper Birch

Called inside for supper, my daughter
tells me I'm almost there. Out past

where my foot won't trust a branch
a ream of paper waits. At thirty

feet up in the tree, I'm not as spry
as I used to be. When I see her

glance up at me I idle, unable to decide.
Caught in the strange hymn

of a father's promise, here I am
shimmying toward a strand of peeled bark,

every failed effort gleaned in why.
It's right there. This moment

it's crumbling in her hair.

The Renter Mows His Lawn

Out in the backyard on a Saturday morning
I'm sweating through the tee
just enough

to wake neighbors. Ripping the cord
towards me over and over

I'm unsure why it won't listen,
won't wake to the song of domestic despair.

With the party only hours away
I ask for help,

this haggard nest sprawling,
begging to be cut.

*

Deterred by rock, trunk, and flying stick
I settle in, find the yard's pulse
in patterned order.

Vibrations whisper through forearms and thumbs.
I'm thirty and this is the first time
I've mowed a yard alone.

*

Cutting the grass
I know it's time to make the vow.

Lord, though this is my prayer,
a yard full of half-finished geometric nightmares,

do not despair. For You
I'd take the slow swinging sickle,
unchain the motor and
allow my heart to complete the work
with knife, nail, or grazing tooth.

Parable

Ever since we moved from Cedar Street
whenever there's a lull in my attention,
whenever her baby sister cries,
my daughter retreats alone.
Repelled to the kitchen table,
she draws the curtain and looks outside.
What are you looking for? I ask her.
She never replies.

*

Today, when she moves to the window,
I tell her a story. Slicing an apple
I carve a parable within a parable.
She doesn't want to eat the fruit,
but when I lift the seed from its core,
its black note on the knife,
a brilliant song erupts. We could plant a tree,
I say. *Where?*
she asks. Pointing all around me
and then towards her heart
everything is limitless again:
Here or here or here.

Orange Slivers on the Nightstand

Once she peeled an orange
and offered it to me

not because I said I was hungry
but because she knew I was.

She whispered love
into my ears, and somewhere in this

reverie, I was consumed by the scent
of an orange lingering on her hands.

Everything I do, a reply
to the scent of her fingers upon the fruit I won't eat
                                    unless she peels,

the love I can't understand without my heels
upon her ankles
like broken stanzas that will never be written.

As I rest between her thighs, her fingers brush my hair,
comb through my anxiety of hidden statues

emerging from the Yellow Sea.

Deep within the wood,
I am polishing my sadness for her

and she is so patient. For the labors we have fought for,
for our love that has grown upward,

facing the sun,
        I can see tiny orange slivers on the nightstand, sitting still,

waiting for me,
while she runs her orange-soaked hands through my graying hair.

Amen

Alone in an empty parking lot
it happens. For a long time
I thought this steel voice

rising in me might be
explicable, its static song
a side effect of a metal cheek

that caused radio signals
to scatter into busted beads,
into a thread of light I followed

toward the Lord. Shiver.
Shiver to know we're closer,
we've moved past

our own illusion. Traveling
the length of my body's fatigue,
I've counted, repaired, and

reissued every *Amen*
that dissolved the instant
before my tongue spoke it.

I've stripped its melody,
made it plain: *so-be-it*
I said without self-regard.

The sky, you should know,
is a voice and weather
is its morpheme.

When I go to the sacred place
past the long knee-high grass
of my mother's sorrow

to the end of me, to
a coast I've never seen,
I say your name

over and over and over
because I'm terrified
I will forget it. I say

Amen, but its end stop
is never final and
nothing is *so-be-it.* Nothing

in this world owns that collar,
an electric spark
shocking us whenever

we cross borders of debate.
Open to me, Lord,
the golden thread,

a wire streaming through
all my brokenness
until it rises

and is dusted, counted, and sorted
for Your good. Here I am,
unsure what's faster:

the speed of my thoughts or
the speed of the hand
that casts its buzz.

Electricity zipping through trees,
zeroing in on me
through my first chill of winter,

isolates where my doubt can rise,
frees praise I've denied
and forced underground:

Amen.
Amen.
Amen.

Touchdown

When I go to Korea,
I won't take much:

just a football.

Guiding each child's hand,
I'll teach them

to celebrate, to feel
as free as I do.

Spike it, I'll say.
Like this.

Notes

"Loran" – A navigational radio system used by United States Navy to locate any position through its proximity to other fixed locations.

I.

"Mother Tree" – Korean culture is defined by active nationalistic mythologies. Koreans believe that their founder, Tan'gun, created their nation's first dynasty over 2,300 years B.C. Tan'gun's father was the son of the emperor of heaven and his mother was a woman who had been transformed from a bear.

"Pushing Chi" – A Tai Chi move, whereby the practitioner, attempts to "push and pull" energy to and from his or her body.

"Aureole" – Aurora is the goddess of morning.

"Hikikomori" – A socio-cultural phenomenon whereby youth become paralyzed by their own perception of failing their parents, their societies. In some, the damage is so severe they do not leave their rooms or only take to the streets at odd periods of the night for fear of meeting others or provoking conversation. I first became alerted to this term in an article in *The New York Times Magazine*.

"Land of the Morning Calm" – An ambiguous term possessed by both North and South Koreans alike. It has some connection with the title Christian missionaries used for Korea in the nineteenth century.

"One Hundred Words for Snow" – The adage that yields some truth. In some Inuit tribes, the word "snow" can be described in many different degrees or types.

II.

"Two Thousand Lilacs" – Highland Park, located in Rochester, New York, holds one of the nation's largest displays of lilacs in May each year.

III.

"Sea Woman" – Haeyno, in Korean society, is a professional diver who plunges into waters in search of seafood.

"Breaking News" – Anapji Pond is a national landmark and treasure in a south eastern province of South Korea. The garden was recreated to match the design of the original.

IV.

"Blue Periods" – Juche, a nationalistic mantra of North Korea, translates as "Self-Reliance" and places rigorous demands on each citizen to help strengthen the nation under its political leadership.

"Orange Slivers on the Nightstand" –Disputed borders along the 38th parallel create frequent debate over ownership of particular territories in the Yellow Sea.

Acknowledgements

For their acute and keen reading of my early drafts of these works, I thank all my friends at Spalding University, but especially Debra Kang Dean, Amy Watkins, Dave Harrity, and Jonathan Weinert.

I also am grateful to the editors of the following publications where the following poems were first published, some in slightly different forms:

Buffalo News: "Word," "Reincarnation," and "Heading Westward at 495 mph," published originally as "First Date with my Second Daughter"

Rock & Sling: "River" and "Song: Decade"

Tulane Review: "Hives"

Saranac Review: "Postage"

Bellingham Review: "Collage of Seoul"

Penwood Review: "Hikikomori" and "Aureole"

Korean Quarterly: "Apartment near Airport" and "Land of the Morning Calm"

Heartland Review: "Pushing Chi"

Ruminate: "Doors among Trees" and "Wired Jaw"

Blood Lotus: "Two Thousand Lilacs"

Louisville Review: "Canticle" and "Orange Slivers on the Nightstand"

Tiger's Eye: "Loran" and "Unnamed"

Ontologica: "Passports" and "Artifacts"

Acknowledgements

Relief: "Parable," published originally as "The Apple Seed"

The Cresset: "Windsock"

Minnetonka Review: "Mother Tree"

Perihelion: "Touchdown"